Myra Schneider was born in London in 1936, and spent her childhood during the war years on the Firth of Clyde. She studied English at London University, and now teaches multi-handicapped adults at a day centre in North London. Among her publications are four poetry collections from Littlewood, most recently *Crossing Point* (1991), and three novels for children and teenagers from Heinemann. Her poems have appeared in many magazines and newspapers, including *Critical Quarterly, London Magazine, The Observer, Poetry Wales* and *Quadrant* (Australia), and also in such anthologies as Virago's *Chaos of the Night*.

MYRA SCHNEIDER

Exits

ENITHARMON PRESS LONDON
1994

First published in 1994
by the Enitharmon Press
36 St George's Avenue
London N7 0HD

Distributed in Europe
by Password (Books) Ltd.
23 New Mount Street
Manchester, M4 4DE

Distributed in the USA
by Dufour Editions Inc.
PO Box 449, Chester Springs
Pennsylvania 19425

ISBN 1 870612 44 2

ACKNOWLEDGEMENTS

Poems from this collection have appeared in:
*Ambit, Aquarius, The Blue Nose Poets Anthology, The Bound Spiral,
Critical Quarterly, Envoi, Foolscap, The Frogmore Papers,
The Inquirer, Iron, The Lancaster Literature Festival Anthology 1992,
Klaonica, Poems for Bosnia* (Bloodaxe), *London Magazine,
The Observer, Odyssey, Orpheus* (Bulgaria), *The North,
Poetry Durham, Poetry Wales, Quadrant* (Australia), *Seam,
Vision On* (Ver Poets Competition Anthology 1992).

'The Three Men', 'Root Vegetable Stew', 'Giving' and 'Signs' were
prizewinners in the Aberystwyth Open Poetry Competition 1991,
the Lancaster Literature Festival Poetry Competition 1992 and
the Bournemouth Open Poetry Competition 1993.

'Pigeons' was broadcast in *Stanza* on Radio 4.

The Enitharmon Press gratefully acknowledges a grant from the
London Arts Board towards the production costs of this volume.

Set in 10pt Walbaum by Bryan Williamson, Frome,
and printed by
The Cromwell Press, Broughton Gifford, Wiltshire

Contents

In the Beginning

Wheatflakes in a chestnut-brown bowl, thinking
slowed down by sleep: the morning is the same
as any other. But no repeat is exact —
the cloud cover is thicker/thinner, skin
a day more creased, closer to dust.

And this morning is marked by tufts of sparrow
on the floor: the machine that laced a small body
with blood has been stopped. The postman's late.
Headlines exclaim from the paper. When I put on
the right glasses I discover today is momentous.

Scientists have discovered the big bang they believe
set off the universe. Trying to follow, I soon
flounder among technical terms, am rescued
by the tulips standing on the breadcrumbed counter.
Their parrot scarlet sings and sings in my head.

If I'm to get a grip on time and space
I must widen my field of vision. Outside,
car tyres hiss. As drivers slow
at the roundabout they'll read: 'Jesus is alive',
chalked in pigeon-dropping white on a support

of the railway bridge. I question this slogan
as I swoop underneath in my crimson Mini estate…
If I'm to understand I must study sciences
for decades, and focus on a past before bridges
arched, before Jesus walked on water,

before ape men squatted in caves,
before dinosaurs lumbered,
before leaves fleshed steaming forests,
before rocks hardened,
before the Earth was flung into orbit round the Sun,
before the birth of galaxies now burnt out,
before matter scattered.

Warm fingers black with newsprint, I tremble
at the dark and shapelessness before the beginning,
the mystery of something grown out of nothing,
the changes that led to the kickstart moment
when space ballooned and time began.

Today has shrunk too small to tackle but from habit
I pour Go Cat for the murderer. A petal
falls. The post flaps onto the mat. I pick up
your letter, and suddenly nothing in the universe
is more important than reading your words.

Cupboards

You enjoy binning tins with rusted rims,
being ruthless with a packet of split peas
beyond its date, and sugar-wrinkled currants
clinging together; you sink a jar scrawled
with peanut butter in a bowl of soapy water.

Rubber-gloved, you lean across a shelf
to wipe out grime with a cloth doused
in primrose freshness, remember a shining
black box high as your shoulders, pulled
from a step-in cupboard onto lino floor,

remember the fidgeting as musty summer frocks
were pressed to your ribs to see if they would fit.
In that cupboard you hid from grown ups, crawled
through to the eaves, searched floorboards
for diamonds, summoned an ark for your woolly animals,

invented codes for worlds that can't be pinned
to words. Now, your cubby hole is in your head.
It holds a thornless garden, a gentle face
you must touch and touch, fruit skins,
stones you can't crack; and in a wicker basket

your teddy bear wan with age, old pains
still glittering and sharp as pins.
Everything's matted as the mesh round unwinding
cotton reels. You try to separate a skein,
end up with a handful of useless threads.

But these shelves you've cleaned are solid,
contained by door and wall. Easing crinkles,
you smooth new flower-scrolled fablon,
line up your glass and plastic bottles
in beautiful rows, block the world outside

where your role is to stare at a screen
as sirens mow streets, countries are carved up,
children with legs thin as the rods
of angle-poised lamps, hobble on ragged ground,
and full-bellied planes are stranded on runways.

In this small area *you* are the decision-maker.
By filling a clear jar with lentils you make
an orange-flecked sun. Like contented faces
lids gleam. For minutes you find comfort
in your realm of cupboard. Then hands invade.

Considering the Aubergine

A snugly rounded pestle, shiny
as the wet curve of a dolphin,
dark imperious purple. It silences
tomato, calls up ceremonial elephants
treading India's dust.

'I could kill for aubergines!' – my son.
His last craze was carrots.
I chop the white flesh
that will soon be stirred with onions,
cumin, crushed garlic.

'Who was it?' I asked in my dream,
these drop earrings for giants
dangling from my head, my voice
full-bodied, my heels
stamping on a granite smile…

The salted pieces lie
in my dented colander. If only
the jug's cool earthenware
weight could squeeze out
all our bitterness with theirs.

Root Vegetable Stew

For Carole

When dark nights eat up afternoons
I sweat onions in sunflower oil,
weigh out carrots, a swede,
and tapering baby parsnips
with old-age skins on flesh
that fattened underneath the light
in a cradling of clay, grit, stones.

I take the swede, a misshapen globe
marred with scars, cut it in two.
The apricot bulk makes my head
hum with summer. I slice up
the snow-white parsnips, then tip
lentils, seeds of a butterfly-
petalled plant, into the pan.

Opening the door to throw peelings
in a pail, I bump into snouting cold.
It smells of woodsmoke, bites
as I stare at the park bristled
with black. Frost is stiffening leaves,
grasses, and I feel myself woven
to this land's Saxon past when winter

was a giant who trampled crops in fields,
snuffed breath with icicle fingers –
though this was not the country
of my forbears, though rootlessness
was a wound I bore till turned thirty,
I was warmed enough by love
to put down roots in myself.

When chill sinks its teeth in my ribs,
I retreat to the stove, dip a spoon.
The heat-swollen lentils are melting
among the hulking vegetables,
and yellowbrown as November woods.
I add lemon and fried spices,
stir them in, ladle the stew.

The Three Men

Three strange men
have risen from the pale beds
of nearby gardens. I peer
through a cleared pane
at their bodies stiff with moonlight,
and cold fishbones my spine.

The three seem to be behind
the feathered quiet that's turned
distant trees blue
as lips unfed by blood.
Was it their idea to write
bawling war slogans

across a park wall in snow
that petrified on the red bricks?
Standing in the herbaceous border
I scratched with my capped biro,
couldn't erase one letter of:
'Get the bastards in their tanks!'

The three figures have the bulk
of pillars, of fear. One
is wearing a bucket hat
but they confront
the steely air coatless,
commune mutely with the moon.

The serrated icing has dropped
off fences and feet have rumpled
the park's soft blankets.
Where tyres have stamped themselves
in sludge I watch black snow
slipping into an inky puddle.

The whiteness has shrunk to nothing
but in nearby gardens
are three tumbled torsos,
three yellowish lumps ·
of slowly wasting matter,
a bucket on its side, grass.

A Letter to Sujata in Bremen

You've been here, seen the frilled curtains,
the diamond panes in Morton Way,
and all the trees restrained on verges.
But I must imagine Mozartstrasse,
the house where you live, your landlady.
Is there a girl on the floor above yours
who sits at a piano playing tunes
from 'The Wonder Boy', a book I was given
when I was eight? I can hear
'Eine kleine Nachtmusik' – its notes,
clustered droplets of light sparkling
on the ceilings and walls of tall rooms.

And suddenly – you'll smile at this –
my mouth is watering, my head's crammed
like a shop window in Salzburg,
with boxes of Mozartkugeln, each
gold-papered and stamped with a picture
of the genius fastened in tight lace,
in a jacket red as haws.

Do you know these chocolate globes?
Of course they have nothing to do
with the giddy living, the intensity,
the rush of patterned sounds to the brain;
nothing to do with the envy, the complaints
about too many notes, the fluctuating success.
Or Mozart dying, maybe poisoned
by his medicine, with poverty at the door.

So I knew my sketches
of 18 Mozartstrasse were only fantasies
even before I read your story
about the damenschneider who lived
and worked at your address before the war,
who sent his Jewish wife to America,
who disappeared along with his scissors,
cottons, sewing machine. Nothing remained
but pins and needles littering the floors.
Those days so many thinned into air,
leaving neither wisp nor whisper.

14

As my childhood ended – years before
you were born – scraps began to surface
about the cruelty to Jews in the War.
I stuffed the horror under the carpet,
buried guilt inside myself,
trembled that I was a Jew.

And even now, Sujata, I turn off
documentaries about concentration camps,
afraid terror will march through my sleep
and wakefulness for the rest of my life.
Yet there are sentences I've read
that are red-hot needles embedded in me:
'Every person had one small bowl
to eat from, drink from, piss in.
We washed ourselves in our urine.'
'Mothers were made to watch…'

I try to imagine someone
who's tortured women and children,
going home, kissing his daughter,
moved to tears by a piano concerto.
I fail…

But here is a fragment that's survived
all the years since 1941:
Frau Schneider, my husband's grandmother,
stick thin, widowed, eighty,
was dragged from her flat in Vienna.
Wedged between the jeering neighbours
was the daughter who'd been astute enough
to bury her identity and resurrect herself
with blonde hair and Christian names.
Mouth full of helplessness, she watched
her screaming mother borne away…

This sub-zero December morning
I take an envelope out of a drawer,
write your address: 18 Mozartstrasse,
think of Cherubino's questioning song,
its notes that flutter and stab ecstasy;
the bittersweet weavings of violins,
how the clarinet soars trilling light.
Then I shiver and touch my pale flesh
– how many lost tailors, how many
last sightings of grandmothers?

Pigeons

The morning is swallowed by its headlines:
an old man in Bosnia shot as he scurried
along a path to feed his pigeons.
I try not to see the open mouth
jutting from a black heap of coat.

Going into a room upstairs, I remember
two white pigeons I saw in Ravenna.
How they startled with life,
orange claws gripping the stone rim
of a bowl on a wall in a mausoleum.

For fifteen centuries one has dipped
its beak to drink cool aquamarine;
the other's turned towards a cobalt sky.
What will soothe the cooped pigeons?
In a book I look at the hundreds of tesserae,

follow the shadow lines beneath
wings, the breasts shaped by fingers;
think of two hands blue-rivered
with veins, papered with skin, cupping
the feather softness over beating hearts.

Then I see faces grazed by fear,
slippered feet scrambling up a hill,
a bag of seed split and scattered,
birds' wings frantic behind mesh,
an old man coffined in mud.

The End of the Year

If I ease the curtains round
the curves of the bay, slide them together,
I'll erase the day that's dimming already.
But I'd shut myself in with the small
routines of cups and saucers, problems
I can't solve, unanswered letters,
the radio harping on storms, depressions –
and shrink to Alice at the table's foot.

In the street it's not dark yet;
dusk flowers over my thoughts.
Frost has creased gardens, laced
stems notched with yellow jasmine,
furred roofs. In a brick frontage
glass eyes hold miraculous warmth
like a face I love. Bells begin,
swing stars of sound through the air.

Beyond iron gates the park lies
pale blue and quiet as death.
To keep the day I walk westwards, glad
to be with myself – the jigsaw that's me.
Seeded with the last of the light,
I remember how I used to put a bulb
red as burning coal in my child's room
to plant safety at night, turn for home.

You remember *grow* – one hand rising
between the thumb and finger-cluster
of the other, echoing leaves unfolding
and petals opening as the wrist emerges?

I'll slide my arm through, cradle
my elbow in my palm – now you're looking
at the branching trunk of the king of plants.
You love these neat connections

so pinch your thumb and middle fingers
into a snout, raise first and fourth
to ears – you're laughing at the animal mapped
with brown that grazes tree tops.

I add a small leaf to my twigs –
leaves signpost the shape of the year.
Next week: the leafless season;
we'll pull *cold* across our ribs,

hunt the dark months in your diary.
In April you'll write about green leaves
on trees pink with flowers; by September
you'll quell the whole year with labels.

You'll never describe the green singing
in the blood, the smell of July in a river
of willows, the appalling fall of red
and yellow, grief standing naked.

But your face pale with intent,
your tumbling laughter, that hoard
of signs and words you struggle to gather,
labour to keep – all these
speak tellingly as trees of seasons.

Becoming

Today we'll fold up wheelchairs,
ignore brains with faulty settings,
slip out of strapped feelings,
and let felt tips loose
on these alluring white sheets.

Dan, undersized, his face
stiff as the leather glove he wears
to hide misshapen fingers,
is turning into a giraffe slabbed
with orange. His crane neck lifts
his mouth to a bundle of angular leaves.

Muris, who is deaf, fights
unruly limbs, signs 'afraid'
against his chest. Seizing a pen,
he almost tumbles, rights himself,
steers a pair of erratic saws
across the paper and to emphasize
they're jaws, bangs one arm down
on the other. Gleeful predator now,
he mimes gobbling me up.

But he can't squeeze my bulk
between his teeth. From the head
I've scrolled in violet I uncurl a trunk
and ears generous as banana fronds.
Letting go of fears that still
shallow my breath, shrink me behind
flesh walls, I mountain a back,
plant myself on pillar legs.

Though my weight would shatter scales
I tread neatly as a ballerina.
My small eyes miss nothing.
My long elastic limb traces
the soft swell of ripening fruit,
lavishes the river's liquid jewels
on heads, fondles hides.

No longer threatened,
I fill my tusks with cherry pink.
Dan points; Muris shrieks
with delight; everybody laughs.

Within Grasp

A furred drizzle hiding the sea,
the hill tedious with stone walls,
so she lagged behind Mummy and the pram
filled with grizzling baby.
Nothing delicious except the dandelions
in the grit outside the Merrylees',
each perfect as an unbroken yolk.
Fingers could never reach
the bottom of all that yellow...

'Not a nice flower!'
She trudged beneath her mother's arms,
strapped to disappointment, stretched
to be a mother too. The pram
threatened to roll her down the twists
to the shore racked with weed
but she bumped it a few steps,
then elbows breaking, gave in;
was a nothing again.

The sun was out the afternoon
she and Eleanor pulled all
the yellow heads. Hands stickied,
they were touching the closing faces
when Mr Merrylees loomed,
severe as a steeple. She fled home,
knowing nothing in the world
could prise the petals open again.

Light came in the night, took her
down her garden. A feather seed,
she floated over the hedge,
by leek and cabbage rows to a stairway
into the gound where darkness was velvety
as a party dress. In seconds
she slid out by the sea, saw
its wildness was combed, its grey
crayoned blue. On the water
jewels grew and the cups painted
with silkclad ladies she'd seen
once in a strange window.
And scattered over sea and beach
were flecks bright as dandelions.

Honor's Tree

Two lines, inches apart,
run from top to bottom
of the page,
moving together a little,
then away again –
a trunk that houses
four leaves
narrow as pea pods
in its solid body.

Four branches lead off
Honor's tree,
two on each side:
pathways, passages, pipes,
arms held out.

Wadded for years
by wards with lockers,
drugs on trolleys,
doctors with distant faces,

Honor has written about
ordering flowers
for your wedding,
and picking flowers
in a garden where you remember
childhood and the calm
you had from your mother.

In Honor's drawing
one branch bends
like an elbow
and stretches upwards.
Two spidery threads
trail from another.
I touch the leaves
shut in wood,
seed of forests
fluttered by sun.

Hanging Onto Blackberries

For Peter

Laura's caressing voice
turns 'sun' and 'beautiful',
into such sickly sweets –
she's knitting her mother, her aunt,
the field where she picked blackberries
into a rosepink tea cosy.
My fingers itch to unpick
her idyll, push her head
into the sharp outlines of then.

I glance out of the window
at a bramble spur rooted
in a rubbish heap and the years
blow off like thistle seeds.
I'm seven, excitement tugging me
between barbed wires,
no wrongness running up my spine;
grown ups are occupied with bags
and sticks, and Mummy's wearing
her best mood, not jabbing
pointed words into me.

As I run along paths that web
the hillside's bush and furze,
a warship honks far below
on the wide grey Firth.
Crouched in flaccid grass
I spot a branch crammed
with berries, each cluster
of jet seed pearls
loose in its prickly hasp.

Hands and mouth stain
as I cull into shining glass.
And at last the glory of filling
my first jar, tipping it
into a basket pale as wafers.
I battle with stems, bear wounds
proudly as V for victory,
plan to go on picking for ever.

The end is stamped with a feast
of sardine and jam sandwiches,
fairy cakes – everything
iced with out-of-doors.
Mothers' faces are dusted
with smiles; not a trace
of the unquenchable fire
that can light up Mummy's eyes,
burn me through and through –
for asking, not asking,
for losing my hair ribbons,
flicking my sister...
This afternoon perfection
is a balloon that stays afloat.

On the heavy kitchen scales
the arrow points to pound
after unrationed pound.
The mountain in the silver pan
sinks with its snowcap of sugar;
ripeness fills the whole house.
If I close my eyes berries
wink in my head's dusky sky.

All night mush seeps
through the jelly bag
that's thick as my liberty bodice.
When the bottles are sealed
I skate my fingers on the circles
of cellophane sleek as ice,
clasp the glass, sure of the purple,
tongue-smooth sweetness, inside...

Face fogged by loneliness,
Laura's waiting for me
to speak. I offer the tick
she needs for comfort. She smiles,
a pasty child with a lollipop –
I want to keep my vision intact.

Latin Lessons

Our grizzled Latin primer began
by conjugating love: 'amo...amas...'
I found it satisfying inflecting gender,
tense, mood. Later I was excited
by Vergil's long images; but Miss Crook,

a thin spinster with lank threads,
had cheeks wasted as winter, a voice
that droned hexameters and explanations
while her fingers performed contortions
on the desk. I knew love hadn't fed
her jutting neck, her crotch, her heart.

Teetering in socks and check dress,
I longed to be kissed, propped my self esteem
by mocking her saplessness; at home
tried to stop the red-hot jaws
that opened when my parents quarrelled
from eating into my bedroom, snapping me up.

Once, collecting for a charity, I called
at her house. A small creature in its lair,
she lay among books and muddle
reading Horace. I wondered what they meant
to her – the words I lapped that wooed
Lydia, the playfulness entwining vines.

I too escaped in books. Shocked,
I tried not to breathe the loneliness
souring the walls as she dropped
money in my tin. The narrow windows
stared out at wind-shaken beeches.

Finding Audrey

'Do you know where Audrey lives?'
Her eyes plead;
her hump's a heavy sack
for her slight, breathless body.

'I'm sure her house is by the park
but I can't find it.'
Her skin is netted with veins,
nose tip raw red,
eyes watery, and her arms flounder
inside a big, grey coat.

She points at ungainly semis,
brick decoration blurred
in the thin mist. I can't produce
the answer she wants to prise,
apologise. She scuttles over the road.

On the railway bridge her hope
is still flailing in my head.
Has she forgotten Audrey's dead,
been misled, muddled this piece
of street in Palmers Green
with one of a thousand lookalikes?

If I helped her search
what hours of twisting ways,
doublebacks, cul-de-sacs,
would snare me?

Light is running along
the train tracks, leaping off
the pale heights of Alexandra Palace.
A few leaves cling to branches.

Let Audrey open a painted door,
lead her to the hothouse in the park
to be bathed in the deep green
of fringed banana fronds,
the magenta of primula petals
and the quivergold of fat fish
at the foot of the tiny waterfall.

Finding Dorothy Wordsworth

For John

I can't take my eyes off
the silver snips of light
fish-flicking the lake's surface.
By these trees you hurried to Rydale,
hoping for letters from your brother.
One night the moon shone
like herrings in the water.

The white lines chalked on the fell
are your Milk Churn Force.
I climb towards the waters' roar;
and suddenly froth streams are tumbling
down stone rifts; sound fills my head.
Breathless, at the head of the gill,
I think of you walking here alone.
You saw purple light on Silver How, .
knew Helm Crag as a being by itself.

Pilgrims queue to see the mould
you used for making candles,
wet flagstones in the larder.
It needs your words to stir life
into Dove Cottage: 'I mended stockings...
William composed without success...
I read Paradise Lost...O the darling!
Here is one of his bitten apples!
I can hardly find it in my heart
to throw it in the fire.'

Outside, quiet grows in the plot
where your brother planted rows of peas,
in the orchard where he liked to write,
and you sat watching butterflies
through each other's eyes, pooled
thoughts and feelings –
the love between you an intensity
closer than blood or bond.

In the steep lane behind the cottage
where you gathered mosses to make
the chimney gay for your darling's return,
cars bull past. I touch
stones cushioned with moss.
Once you tried to soften
his absence by sleeping in his bed.

Not a word in your notebook
of William's engagement to Mary.
The night before the wedding you slept
with the ring on your finger,
next morning took it off
but your brother slipped it on again.

You watched the couple walk down
the avenue to the church, shut
your feelings inside the house.
But when you knew it was over,
hopelessness unstoppable as love,
spilled out and you threw yourself
on your bed, lay neither hearing
nor seeing until you were told
they were coming back, then you forced
yourself out into the October air,
fell upon William's bosom,
welcomed dear Mary.

That March you'd seen the moon
hung high over Silver How
like a gold ring snapped in two.

Au Salon de la Rue des Moulins

(a painting by Toulouse-Lautrec)

The smudge-pink negligée is a refuge.
Its standing collar hugs your neck
but the thin silk exposes
your nakedness: knees, small belly.
Warmth breeds among the cushions –
look how loosely the others
are holding unclad shoulders –
but cold shudders your back
as you press stiff hands together.
Your hair done in a fetching topknot,
green in this light, softens
your taut cheeks. You've coloured lips,
not learnt to paint out feelings.

I could turn from your sadness
and unwind in the plum-mauve sofas,
the pink panels, the blue ribs of columns,
the arching black of Gothic passages.
But the carved gilt is gaudy,
and there's a reek of perfume laced
with the smell of unwashed bodies.

Besides, I can't take my eyes
from your white face or the cheeks
rouged to hide crumpling skin,
or the black stockings of the sprawled girl
who is nursing a shapely knee.
At the back, beneath a hoisted slip:
a stark thigh, buttock creases –
I'm ashamed to be here – forget
I'm an intruder in this crimson palace
as I breathe in the listlessness
of vacant women unfed by daylight.

And you? Like the others you expect
to be used again and again
until you can't smooth over decay
with creams, and you're crossed off –
goods not worth hiring out.
You clutch at a fine-handkerchief dream
of a saviour who will take you away
to airy rooms sweet with lavender,
where you'll pour love on one another,
soothing as warm water from a ewer.

This tawdry place, its business
bruises. In your eyes the hurt
of so many women. It cries out in me.
But there's tenderness here too.
The slut in the pale blue shift –
the one so easy in black stockings –
is leaning towards you, smiling
and trying to gentle out the pain
stitched deep into your body.

The Scream

Cries scrape the darkness,
split my sleep –
in the thickness of trees
fox or owl must be
twisting a neck.
A madness of risen fur,
feather, claw
fills the night.

In my body's warm bag
I lie close
to guilt, willing
the pain to cease.
The slaughterer seems too large
to be confined to flesh,
spans the earth,
its face a moon's stare.

The noise becomes a girl's
squeals in the distance.
It must be foolery
in the park – a chase
threading the viaduct's
arches. I wipe out
grass-soiled hands
chopping at breath.

Then silence pesters,
invents shrieks muffled
by walls' cool
Chinese scenes.
I think of the scream
jammed so deep
it can't fly to the throat,
only reflect in the eyes.

In the morning I struggle
from throttling dreams,
walk down the path,
search the lawn
flattened by leaves
wide as open palms,
for tufts and bones
stained with blood.

Treeless

In her childhood too few trees.
Only hawthorns elbowed and brambles
clawed at the edges of the field opposite.
Tallest in her garden, the fuchsia bush
which tempted with crimson-cloaked ladies.

She undid their purple skirts, then ran
from Mrs Guild next door – her white
shrivelling silence – to dig in the rut
by the sandpit, hoping gold might smile
when she reached the far side of the world.

It was a trek to the wildness where branches
thrilled the bluster sky with leaves,
to the forest of firs so tensely woven
no person could unravel paths,
only the witches she pulled out at night.

On the hill up from the Firth was a tree
the bigger children climbed. One day
a girl pushed and hauled her up its trunk.
Terror beating her wooden body,
she gaped at the swirling distance to the ground,

wanted to hide from the clout of voices,
dangerous faces, blindly found
her way to its comfort. But the tree-dream
was unbroken, pursued her on rocky shores,
on scarps tufted with bell heather.

And she hoarded 'Glorious England' stamped
on cigarette cards, wanted to be that girl
in a long-ago dress cooling her feet
in a stream so full of summer boughs
and darting sun, her body ached.

When they moved South an oak
kinged the long, suburban garden,
and plum trees dropped hundreds
of purpled eggs that cracked, loosing
honeyed green into the dry grass.

And longing swam through her for the sea
that fell ceaselessly upon the shore,
for the wind-flattened ridge
where bogs glinted like devils' eyes,
and pewits cried across the treelessness.

Willows

On grass still flattened and muddied
by winter, gulls stand bleak
as playground swings. I hurry down
to the willows, the first trees to green,
the last to yellow. By the Brook
one is stooped like a mother
over the hump of wooden bridge.

I walk in the stillness beneath the twine
of finger leaves, feel a certainty
I couldn't find when I was a child,
and the tea table was a white field
stiff with woven flowers.
Instructions thistled my head: 'Sit up...
remember your manners...the visitors.'

I remember the china petals on the jampot,
talk spreading ease like butter,
my hands peeling paper frills
from a fairycake, anger flaring
in my mother's eyes, ready
to strike when the guests had gone.
Had I forgotten a 'please', a 'thank you'?

The day cracked; its brightness ran.
No way to save myself. Words
fell. Then a fortress face.
For hours I was chained to disgrace
that rubbed me raw while the voice
that lulled with song, the mouth that smiled
stories, held back forgiveness...

The snow-capped cakes, the words
that cut, the white tablecloth, the wound,
shiver into fragments, dissolve...
In the green quiet I'm peering
at pale water that doubles
the dark arch of the bridge to make
a mottled egg I long to hold.

                    * * * * * *

39

From the first day his yells
sliced into my head, and before
my womb subsided, I learnt
to quieten his loud mouth

by running the pram up
and down the park, past
the twisted trees weeping
leaves that clogged the Brook.

I found out the pram was a badge.
It attracted women who cooed,
took it on themselves to turn
the baby, flattened me with advice.

On the phone my mother's voice
was clipped, mine needy.
No cord between us. Chained
to feeding, changing, washing,

I wanted to turn taps,
drown the baby's crying,
yet was frightened his silence
meant his breathing had ceased.

Mother-all-enfolding
and mother-always-on-demand
fought together in my head
as I pushed and rocked and wrung.

* * * * * *

At first I thought
escaping to hospital
would sever me
from motherhood;
spent days
wheeling round
the broken bits of self.

The lawns were smoother
than the grass in the park
but wherever I went
pain needled the air.
Afraid I'd be unstitched
I hid in the numbness
beneath my head's hood.

Grey doctors
dizzied me with drugs,
flicked away my faint words,
made no attempt
to put me together.

One day a girl spoke to me.
Her voice, her face,
her narcissus-pale hair,
pierced my darkness.
She gave me brushes,
a glory of powdered colour.
Suddenly I saw a house,
wanted to hold the baby.
Leaves fountained
in a dip of park.
Trembling,
I mixed turquoise paint,
on paper released
myself.

* * * * * *

This evening it's summer. Light plays
on the playground swings. The Brook
storm-swollen beyond its bounds
last week, slides silkily by.

I run my hands through seedheads
and heavy leaves. The cooling grass
smells sweet as milk, as the love
I've slowly learnt to take in.

41

When the sky whitens and pushchairs
head for home, there is always
a mud-stained child, a dog nosing,
a voice calling. I walk to the path
lit by the globes of low moons,
through the stillness of willow folds.

Being

For Caroline

I should be sorting socks,
checking words, chopping onions.
Stomach queasy,
I lie down on my bed,
stare at the smother of clouds,
at a sycamore branch
that's been naked all summer.
Rain is splintering the windows.

When a rook flies into the tree
it breaks the tension.
I unhook.
News trickles from the transistor
while the cat dreams
on my cream dressing-gown,
and light eases yellow sashes
between the cloud folds.
The phone rings but I don't answer.
Time opens softly as a long-necked flower.

The Dinner Party

For James

I long to slip back to the street
sweetened by the smell of lime trees,
but Rose, our hostess, gaunt
beneath her smile, is leading us
through her studio, past
canvasses of desiccated plants
to join the other guests on the patio.

Two of them I recognize at once
– her fringe and complacent cheeks;
his El Greco thinness, severe
lapels, air of erudition:
the Berkshires, April and Dunbar.
Without a glimmer of recognition
their marble eyes slide over us.

Voice gritty as salted nuts,
Dunbar begins: 'My daughter played
Mozart's Flute Concerto
with butterfly brilliance.
The conductor's accolade was unforgettable!'
Cold salmon lying elegantly
on cucumber waterlilies, is admired,
sliced, swallowed with hock. Rose's
cat appears, sniffs delicately.

Vowels rounded above the fish knives,
April announces: 'I'm going to boast
of my victory over an art dealer in Oxford.'
I note how her fingers fidget
the yoke of her sack-coloured dress
as she works in her son doing
pure mathematics at Magdalen.

Variations on the theme of herbs
are cut short by Dunbar's recital
of their younger boy's remarkable results.
He gives himself a tick for tutoring.
I squirm. Last year Rose's
husband went to a conference
in Brussels, didn't bother to mention
he'd no intention of returning home.
During the storm after the truth struck,
her eldest failed his exams,
crashed her car, is still lame.

Chilled raspberry fool. Rose
spoons it into tall glasses.
Now the Berkshires are in counterpoint,
praising a performance of Rigoletto
staged in a mansion near Maidenhead.
April lets out a neigh of laughter
and suddenly in upper registers,
everyone is name-dropping operas.

The patio resounds with 'exquisite',
'magnificent.' If I said what I think:
'Verdi is suet mixed with sugar',
they'd stone me for blasphemy. So far
my score is nil in this competition.
I search for words to impress
but they flutter out of reach.

Giving up, I watch the cat
chase a paper-thin moth,
then weave her sinuous length
through a bed of tobacco plants
into the chiffon of darkness
to play games with squeaking bodies,
claw throats into silence,
bite off small heads.

Dilys the Cleaning Lady

prickled at the books lying
thick as dust, at the death trap
of flexes in the dining room
where *He* was staring at one
of those computers instead of doing
a proper job in an office.
Hoisting distaste under her overall,
she put on her Marigold gloves.

Upstairs *She* was on the unmade bed
scrawling on paper. No hint
of a dressing-table. In the loo:
postcards of women worse than naked,
and a stain beyond redemption.
She trotted in when Dilys
was scouring the bath's ancient taps.
'In a week or two I'll make these
shine like moons,' she promised,
knowing she wasn't coming back.

Once home, she'd soak off
the morning in a bath fragrant
with orchid essence, dream
of Niagaras of bleach tipping
into sinks, work tops white
as sanctity, and a chrome dazzle
fixed in a flawless sky
obliterating the hordes of ants
always threatening to wriggle
under her door, her skin.

Giving

It takes you so long to rise to your feet
I feel the heave of each heavy ounce
and your body's bewilderment that one side
is stiff as a frostbound towel on the line.

You shuffle-step to an overheated room
where three deaf men are lining up pens,
tracing their picture-thoughts on air. I sign,
tape down your paper, on mine draw

the long blue ribbons of a waterfall, you
at its foot stroking the tight scarlet heads
of chiffon roses on a scarf I gave you.
You sketch a lopsided rock and a face in profile.

I can't extract meaning from your stream
of wordless sounds until a humming begins
in your throat and I realise the rock's a radio.
Your wrists lift to miraculous lightness,

dance knuckles in the air. An African rhythm
sways your trunk, tugs my shoulders and hips.
The deaf men grasp the quickened beat,
finger its fabric, go out wearing smiles.

          * * * * * *

The station is a shell filled with raw
December morning but the scarves hooked
to perches in the Tie Rack's glass cage,
flaunt tropical plumage. I want them all,

choose one with interleaving tongues of mango,
magenta, lavender, ice-pink. As I wrap it round
my neck I know you will laugh at the colours,
pillow your cheek on the polyester silk,

knot it over the woollen band that hides
the unsightly hollow below your crown.
Beyond the taut faces by the departures board
is yours shining through lightless January.

47

Fixing the Beach

We've slipped off backpack time,
can stay all day, paddling in warmth,
staring at the rocks, gigantic arms
that hold this beach and reach
into a green sea swirled with light.

On a boulder we're sharing sandwiches
while you dig at past centuries in a book
and I dip into myself, write to a friend.
Each looks up at a mosaic shore pieced
from different thoughts, feelings, memories.

If I describe the limpet shells
in the shingle, the smell of wet sand
pocketed between seaweed shelves,
the cliff layers with cathedral arches
tongued out, blocks bitten off,
one a whale hulk stranded by the tide,
top perched by kittiwakes,
base prodded by plastic spades –
can I fit this beach into an envelope?

I refocus with binoculars…am wandering
among cairns, on an endless emerald plain,
swinging in blue and glittering space,
bump land again. The lens encircles
a bird with a surprising collar of white
above a grey breast. When it hops
over stones I can't keep it in sight,
skim a handbook without hope –
but there it is – the ringed plover. Lost
in another millennium, you grunt at my scoop.
Lovingly, I commit the bird to paper.
Later my friend will lose this letter,
and I will be hurt, say nothing.

I leave you, turn up my pink
trouser legs. Plunging a foot
into a pool I'm small again,
skirt tucked into school knickers,
netting pincers, staring at tiny
ferocious mouths in a jar, at the eel
I couldn't save from a starfish
that stung it into a dance to death...

We move out of the sun, soothe
salt-dry throats with oranges,
explore the derelict mill on the turf
behind us. The tide's coming in.
Four figures fishing from a ledge
across the inlet, are cut off.
Real or an optical illusion?
I'm panicking when four men with rods
and haversacks march down a steep path,
melt into the calm of the afternoon.

Sea and shadow re-compose and re-compose
the beach. I take my small rucksack,
put away sand-encrusted socks,
my exaltation over the ringed plover,
three folded pages of letter.
The wind burns our backs as we climb
past pungent thyme and thistle beds,
skirt a stubble field where black flakes
from smoke are blown into our eyes.

Tobago Airport

For Jane

It dozes in fields. Chickens
strut on its winding road.
Inside, no luggage carousels –
but pale blue loos
perfect as birds' eggs.

Out on the grass verge
a woman magnificent in yellow
clucks till we cross
to her trestle table, croons
over her sesame sweets.

This airport doesn't shrink me;
and the island's filled my head
with grapefruit trees, verandas,
wide tongues licking
sands soft as paradise.

On the small viewing platform
I reach for the golden ball
of the sun as it falls
from a luminous sky through
sashes of party pink,

begin to believe I won't be
sealed in a tube where earth
and sky are thinned to images
on a screen, and reality's served
neatly on plastic trays.

When the great wings whirr
the man with phosphorescent sticks
is below me, so near I stem
from his shoulders, discover it's me –
I'm flagging in the giant bird!

Pressing knees to its sides
I slot into the body. Air
swings into my face as I lift
to the gathering dusk, grasp
stray tufts of cloud,

glide swiftly over the strip
of darkening water, over fields
of wavy green sugarcane
now invisible, towards
constellations of flutter lights.

The Mango

lies cool in the palm of my hand,
egg of a mythical bird. It's reddened
like a path over the Caribbean Sea
I tried to catch in the camera's box.
Cutting into this fruit tonight

I'm slicing the sun. Its gorgeous flesh
is yellow and boned by a stone flat
as an oar. I hold up a sliver – it shines
in the darkening blue of the windowpane.
Juice drips from elbow and chin.

'You must eat a mango in the bath,'
said the old lady shut in a dim
upstairs flat in a cathedral city
in England, after a lifetime
of Trinidad's sprawling heat.

The pulp is more generous than peach,
rich as laughter, carries a trace
of jasmine, melts my mouth. I'm feeding
body and mind on mellowed sun.
If this were religion I'd believe it!

Cows Crossing

In my mind: our contented silence
as cow after unhurried cow filed
over the road, the farm dogs nipping
backsliders on the verge as they savoured
cocktails of vetch and ragged robin,
then the collie hurrying to boss
us and our camera back into the car.

I wanted our photograph to catch
the sun piercing the morning's fur
and licking dry the white straggles;
the windblown farm woman in wellingtons
caked with earth; the grainy dampness
we breathed as haunch and flicking tail
disappeared up a mud lane.

That day as we drove by cattle
cooling under willows in Gloucestershire,
I thought of our stay in Caribbean heat
spiced with jasmine, coconut palms,
the kiskadee's repeated teck-a-boo,
and recognised how I'd pined for grass
moist as cows' furling tongues.

In the photograph the dogs are insignificant,
each cow flank an atlas page.
Wedges of black continent fitting
into small triangles of southern sea,
are followed by a brown archipelago
trailed across an ocean of white.
The maps are moved by legs with two
lifted hooves curved as question marks.

Choose

I mime easing a closefitting glove
onto the stem of one finger, then another.
With ease you pick up the sign
that makes choice look like a game:
heads or tails; this card or that;
a silken smoothing on or a peeling off
to touch sweet strawberry skin.

You're entranced as together we choose
flowers, faces but I'm puzzling out
why I've kept the gloves from my teens
I hated wearing: cotton with dots,
Italian kid, a pair ruched to the elbow –
finery that preserves hands
from men's grasp, from roughskin life.

I wanted to believe this word packed
with possibility would widen your span.
But as you decide on a cake, a colour,
I'm forced to see there's no 'open sesame'.
Outside the palace where sound hangs
its tapestries in every room you only catch
stray bangs, dull reports.

But many who have no outward flaw
wear handicaps within: crouch
jacketed by anxiety or harnessed
to obsessions career down alleys.
And there are lotteries that can't be fixed
or who would live in a land shrivelled
by drought, a town gutted by war?

Yet though we all end gloved in dark,
possessions lost, we cling to threads
of choice, escape from grey day
by leaping into rainbowed imagination.
Determined to learn, you've crept into
the territory of language, find verges
of flowers many-coloured as Joseph's coat.

The Climbing Frame

It didn't thrill like a sixpenny stick
nailed with twists of red celluloid
that the wind would drive to frenzy,
or curtains rung up for a puppet show.
Unremarkable as the haybox in the kitchen
it was simply a fixture in the garden.

But when we slid between the wooden bars
that divided air into squares,
my sister and I forced our legs
to take gigantic steps above
privet hedges, walls, roofs
to the shaggy-backed moors
and enough blue pieces of sky to stitch
a sailor's trousers into fair weather.

One word could change the climbing frame
from travelling carpet to an orphanage
for our fifteen woolly animals.
Bombed by the Germans, they were bumped
in the dolls' pram down the steep steps
to the home, fed on plasticine sweets.
No danger in this zone from grown-ups
whose tongues inflicted stings that left
hotter, redder swellings than the wasp
that once panicked between my thigh and dress.

Here, we shed the ordinary, a skin dull
as the nursery lino where we squabbled
to stand on the rabbit on the mat.
In this realm no need to change rules
or pinch to win. Adults couldn't touch us
but our touch was fabulous.
We fabricated palaces with domes,
space for both to be queens.

2

The metal climbing frame bells
the air at the end of my lawn
but no children cram its well
or hang, voices ribboning from its struts.
Every minute takes childhood
further away – my own and my child's.

If I stare long enough I see
jerky arms turn into planes,
a tot heaving a bucket of water heavy
as himself to a fire engine's crest;
hear a six-year-old rap:
'you're to have a baby now…'
hear deadly gunfire from twigs
and sudden, shrill resurrections.

3

Today, inside a broken packing case
I found the wooden frame.
On its top, in sunbonnets floppy
as cabbage leaves, sister and I
are perched like Walt Disney flowers.
Nearby, my mother standing higher
than the structure, shrinks it.
How the camera lied!

And the truth is I still need to climb
out of days divided by tensions,
where failure is hunger, success
the power to create destruction,
days when the bodies strewn after battle
don't rise to their feet and walk away,
when faces cracked by grief
merge hopelessly together…
If only I could reach a point
where I could unfold imaginings
to take back to earth through
the frame's airy passages.

Honesty

For Mimi

Coins so thin my thumbs
could flake them to dust,
pods clustered on twigs
fanning a whiteness that crams
the stone mouth of a jar...

Their quiet stills me,
touches the screen's blue folds,
the dressing table's depths,
this room's mirrored dimness.

The rose talcum and hairbrush
belongs to none of us
who borrow cotton gowns
and stretch on the bed
for hands that know the lie
of bones to undo pain from spines.

Landscapes trapped in glass
hang on the walls. Unmoved,
I stare at pools reflecting
perfect trees, mountainsides swathed
in mist, dishonest mauve peaks...

And what is honesty but stepping
from a day where eyes fail to meet
as feet echo by, where passengers
crushed together fail to speak,
keep tight hold of packages?

What is honesty but a slipping
out of clothes to sit alone
with the underself, listening
to its breathlessness
and feeling these silvery skins –
ghosts beautiful as flowers?

Exits

THE ROUNDABOUT

No fairy ring, this!
No curve to prove I'm on a circumference.
If I walked into the small hours
I don't believe I'd reach my starting point.
Nothing blossoms in this wilderness
but concrete spokes, glass petals
and trucks rattling bones down turnings.
I want the comfort of buildings, people.
A grin wide as a football field
slaps my face. It's pasted to a billboard.
I look in vain for a wall behind.

No mulberry bush, this!
No warm hand to thread with mine.
Silent figures pass, faces
tilted, cheeks leached of blood,
skin pewtered by street lights.
Is the twitch in that shadow a mugger,
a rapist? If this were toytown
I'd find a friendly policeman. Ahead,
a flyover soars traffic to the sky.
I listen for the plunge to hell.
Hope is a lost moth swirling.

EXIT ONE

The white buildings glitter
with pinpoints that prick my eyes,
and the cool of morning has dissolved
in heat that snakes up my spine.
My gingham dress is sticky with sweat.

This is not a day to be walled
in an examination hall;
it's a day for running
from pink silk sand through lace of surf
into the sea's salt-green surprise,
for letting the mind float
to a red sail that hangs,
small as a child's flag.

But I'm hooked to an exam
that's been dangling all my life,
and it's in a building I can't find
among these identical blocks.
I run, breath scraping my throat,
slap into the others at the corner.
They're stiff-mouthed as fish
overlapped on a cold slab.
We stream into a rectangular gullet.

Echoing staircases climb
to the weighty hush of an endless hall.
The sun winks at sealed windows,
and the air threatens to dry up.
Precise lines of desks.
On each a paper dark with questions.
Hope is my crushed handkerchief.

When the invigilator fires
the starting gun three years of notes
are torn out of my head.
For years the world has been a dream,
reality confined to analysis,
assessment; flights of imagination,
kingfisher-brilliant flashes,
red-pencilled out.

Gripping my fountain pen,
I scratch in vain at ruled lines.
'Nothing will come of nothing...'
I unscrew the pen at its neck.
The rubber tube is limp,
a body that's leaked its blood...

I look up to find myself outside
a towerblock I recognize – it's decades
since I soared to the silence
that binds the seventh floor library.
My rolled certificate is buried
in a briefcase up in the attic.
And there are days when clusters
of words bloom in my head,
when joy illuminates the world.
But I can't shake off panic:
it flicks; it squirms; it leaps.

EXIT TWO

On a stripped board at a corner: 'Kalamazoo'.
Tiger stripes threading jungle twists?
No, this is Scotland; goosegrey mists
roll back and I slip into a springtime place.

Leaves unknotting are bright as the lime squares
in my paint box. They flutter in a sailor-blue sky,
and we uncover nests of primroses, my sister and I,
layer on layer of petals, fragile hearts.

Marsh marigolds glossy as cupboard doors
in our kitchen, wood anemones with white wings.
We reach into rabbit holes, and each of us sings
and slides wellingtons through grass furred with rain.

Kalamazoo fences us off from fear of missing
the school bus and catching teacher's strap;
from a huge-kneed boy perched with a cap
of stones on a wall, from the nips of weasel girls.

Kalamazoo keeps us from devil shapes in our room
at night; from blue-splinter thorns that voices
thrust deep into flesh; from the wolf faces
that mother and father suddenly put on.

Kalamazoo with silvery bark peeling from birches,
its perfection easy as a bunch of flowers, as the burn
blethering down the hill, will never return.
But in my head it's safe from the spinning world.

EXIT THREE

Fog's edging in. The air's chill
as a churchyard slab. I stare
into a bleak launderette.

A girl with a push chair
shivers in a square of light
thrown by a café window.

'I've nothing – spare a coin!'
Her Irish burr clings; her face
is grey as cold porridge.

Her child's lost in sleep, mouth
ajar. I open my purse –
little comfort in this.

Others press from the dark
with jagged demands. Taking
refuge in 'The Happy Bite'

I breathe greasy warmth, gulp
mouthfuls of soggy doughnut,
can't dislodge the thin girl.

Her hopelessness brings back mine:
days when I peeled potatoes,
foot rocking the crying cot;

how I blubbered that time
the dolls' pram slid from my hands
down a gully in the glen...

Red and sickly, jam spurts.
I see it's the blood missing
from the homeless girl's cheeks

and swill down tea that's thick
with longlife milk to kill the taste;
but it sticks to my tongue.

EXIT FOUR

'The Waving Hand.' This must be the place.
Doors swing into a circus of light
and noise. When I make myself understood
a finger points upwards. In a room
with ginger walls and a flaking mirror
light from fat plastic candles falls
on figures drinking at higgledy tables.

At last a fanfare of clichés from the compère,
and the performer leaps into jokes, knocks sex
as if it were an old coconut, yanks titters
from the audience with a 'fuck' in every line.
The red heart on his sweatshirt proclaims:
'I love myself.' I hate the smallness,
the greed to be big, the gritty upper register.

His smirk hardens to a sneer, his glitter eyes
hypnotise. 'Who do we want to get?' He spins
the smoky room till it rings with 'Gotcha!'
Guffaws of laughter but there's nothing
to laugh at. I tell myself to picture
a meadow with cows but can't keep out:
'I will erase…eradicate…I will purify…'
His name is news on years of papers
that shred and snowflake through my head.
Who would have thought one man
could have so much blood on his hands?

When the audience pelt him with applause
I sneak out, plunge into the dark.
It's quiet as a field on the South Downs
but no larks sweeten the air. At the end
of the street I thrust my weight against
iron gates, enter a wasteland.
Beyond the dull gleam of a rail track
I see blue flames creep over peaks.

What are these hills?
Not earth turfed with grass,
not compressed cars in neat mounds
or old settees, springs like exposed nerves,
not tins mountained into heaps.
I cannot look on these remains.
Bitter smoke infects eyes and skin.
If my voice hadn't stuck in my throat
I'd cry for pink, ribbed sand
washed over and over by the sea.

EXIT FIVE

At last the station with Greek temple columns
and a Gothic tower lording a sky that's sour.
Mid-afternoon but the concourse is as unpeopled
as a desert. Its grey coldness travels through me.
On the departures board all trains are cancelled.
'I'll be late,' I snap, my voice the White Rabbit's.
The stationmaster appears, sniffs my panic, grins:
'Next train at five – passengers will storm it!'

I'm coddling my hands with a paper beaker of coffee
when the train caterpillars in. Doors open.
No scramble. Light entices me into a stuffiness
that's snug. Five-fifteen. Not a whisper of life
on the intercom. Outside, night's clamped down.
Spying a uniformed figure, I tap the glass
but he pretends not to hear. Trains alongside
leave – I'll spend my life on this platform!

When coats have stilled the jumpy yellow lines
on the upholstery I stop crossing out on paper,
talk to the traveller opposite. Her manner's silver
with charm, her face a placid sea. It's no surprise
that her job is pumping money for a heart foundation.
And now the four of us at this table, unfold
ourselves though we're not April pilgrims bound
for Canterbury. It's November and we're going north.

From his small ability to listen I guess my partner
is a retired lecturer. A voice announces over his
with un-British politeness: 'Apologies, track is open
but we are having no driver for your train.' I stab
my sandwich packet with a pen. 'I'll lose the chance
to be heard by hundreds…' The heart lady staunches
my panic with her serenity. A girl in front leaps up,
beaked face scarlet as her jumper. She pulls the cord

above my seat, turns into the red queen. Alarm
rings in the stationary train. The uniformed ones
will brand me with blame, order us off the train
and shuffle us together as if we were nothing
but a pack of cards. An inspector walks down
the aisle. Mouth cemented in disapproval, he gags
the strident bell. At six we creak forwards.
Hope runs up a flag. It flutters in my head –

and droops when we don't budge from a minor station.
'Obstacle on the line'. I fall through tunnel darkness,
am numbed, nothing… 'Track clear as springwater,' sings
the conductor. We race up England; I munch my sandwiches.
Suddenly I'm breathless on a platform, flinging self,
suitcase and notebook into a taxi. I arrive late
but am greeted by thirty people. Words butterfly
from my mouth; alight all over the room.

The orchestra tiny below,
is tuning up. The chessboard
choir is tiered in black
and white. Cockatoo colours
shift among the audience;
programmes fan expectation.

It begins: meadows of sound
where eightsomes of girls weave
a dance. Now they circle,
skirts whirling over the grit
of sadness, faster, faster –
collapse in helter-skelter.

The quiet of straw. I'm watching
a white stream from udders
slipping through fingers. I want
to stay but the pail melts
into the tuba's raised bell,
moon cusps in its liquid gold.

A drumbeat rolls over
the sweep and swell of the violins.
It overwhelms walls, consumes
cattle, people, clouds,
worlds. Nothing left now
but an immense silence.

The small, piercing clarity
of a distant horn. Cymbals
erupt – a procession is upon us:
the dead, feet triumphant;
thousands singing, cheering,
and waving gaudy flags.

I'm inseparable from the silver lips
of flutes, listening faces,
the sounds climbing rungs
to heaven, circling the globe
of light in its dome.
After the last note

it is hard to wear again
the humdrum of body, go down
to a street that's cooled, narrowed.
By a disused warehouse I take
a turning that follows a bridge.
Sacking is hung across an arch,

and through gaps I see
flames leaping madly,
a rope, figures with bottles.
Outside, a girl with a cap
is crouched by a black Labrador,
a mouth organ on her lap.

EXIT SEVEN

Glass doors slide apart, admit me
to 'reception' which has flower arrangements,
the scent of lavender polish, deep settees.
I'm not deceived by this pretence of hotel.

A room to myself. No ward chitter-chatter
but bereft of husband, shoes, suitcase,
in an anonymous gown, I'm lost in the silence,
and the fear girdling me is as tight
as my skin once was over the baby
curled in my body. I blurt my hopelessness
to a nurse who nods: 'Best cough it out.'
Beneath her crisp cap springs a mass
of auburn hair. I long to touch it.

Next morning I'm labelled 'nil-by-mouth'
and at last, the stones in my head swirling,
dissolving, I'm wheeled on a trolley
to a white place where I sense
the shining lines of waiting implements.
Figures robed and masked, surround me.
A jab in my wrist and I disappear.

Worming pain, I escalate downwards,
surface to find I'm beached in bed.
Light leaps, kisses too fiercely.
My arm's grafted to a tree.
Its thin glass branches feed
ruby liquid into my arm. The nurse
with red hair shifts my helpless body.
'A transfusion. You bled like a pig.'
The ceiling see-saws. I close my eyes.
'Don't fret; you'll soon be skipping
like a lamb.' Laughter spikes my ribs.

Days later, pillow propped and separated
from the glass placenta, I drift in and out
of sleep, waiting for the blood
I have received to lace me with strength.
My womb's been taken away,
and sadness tunnels from this finality –
but I'm free now of the curse,
its prologue, disasters banked
above my head. And the aftermath,
energy washed away, body walls
at the point of caving in...

Schubert's Sixth is quicksilvering the piece
of July sky admitted by the open window.
I lower rag-doll legs to the floor,
make a first journey all the way
to the foreign country of the corridor.

EXIT EIGHT

For Kate

Here, wheels are stilled, and boxed fear
can be set free. I unclothe, lie
on a white board. Paper fish float above me,
and the sea seems to unwind as she stirs
essences of lavender, clary sage, rose.

When she smoothes the blanket, cups my head,
I remember the barbed wire enmeshed in the wool
of my mother's warmth, learn to take in
this kindness. Kneading shoulders, she unravels
knots, and tears rise from depths I can't name.

I let her take my elbow's weight, web
her fingers with mine, ease each joint,
and I think of a girl who sat by me once,
the stab of her questions, my sadness when I saw
she was too brittle for anyone to touch.

A circle buds in the small of my back. It opens
upwards, carries the scent of summer pinks.
Lulled from side to side, words come
but no need now to speak. Movement
diminishes to a single dot and I slip

into sleep, press my palm to a face I love.
My whole length is held by friends, their limbs
woven into branches. I surface to the sea-quiet
of her voice, put on shoes, outer self,
go softly through the pounding street.

I don't know how this room occurred
but its mirror is telling fibs –
such silly tufts and the creased cheeks
are dry as greaseproof sheets,
the ones I cut circles from to line
sponge tins. None of this is me.

I want a face I used to wear –
my milk mouth at six, not a curdle in it,
and the bonny smile, all hair-ribbon;
or that sweet-and-twenty me
chock-full of longing to be kissed;
or the topknot worn with dungarees
and my cake-crumb baby on my hip.
Inside, I'm quite as young as then…
only I'm no longer sure the pictures
are me. My brain's unpicked itself
since – since they put me in here.
I'm nothing but finger-fumble now.

Sloppy yoghurt again – take it away!
What I want is to do the tango
with that nice young doctor over there.
He's not a day over fifty,
and he keeps words up his sleeve.
I've seen him get them out.

I've told him a few home truths.
The ones in charge of these old people
like to make believe they're nurses.
Still, they get good marks for kindness.
This morning one took me out
to see the lambs' ears and aubretia
in the rockery. The smell of mown lawn
was perfect heaven. But I want
that green grass with daisy chains
down to the playground.

Yes, I remember the devil roundabout.
I was four, in wellingtons, a gliding queen
until the big boys pushed faster,
faster and the earth giddied
with the sky. My throat screamed
and I plunged from the crazy spin
to the breathtaking punch of ground.
Everything stopped. When I struggled up
my legs were mashed with blood and grit
but I was in solid world again...
Do you know the way back from here?

EXIT TEN

With each heartbeat, each footstep,
the roundabout expands, disclosing turnings.
At its centre half-demolished buildings,
ribs jutting from crumbling sides.
The limbo quiet is jarred by cars
passing with the whirr of birds of prey.

Track lost of time and self,
I strike left at the next intersection.
Morning has cracked the dark's slate,
and seams appear pale as crystal.
Sandals flapping, mind stunned
I run from the grinding juggernauts

to a verge by an old gasometer shell.
In a puddled rut rainbowed with oil,
I stumble on glorious yellow cups
of marsh marigold, a plant that grows
with woundwort and wild cress, needs
to feed on the velvet of stream silt.

Hope rising, I squeeze through a fence
into a yard, pick my way past
roof tiles stacked by planks,
emerge in a back street where jugs,
photographs and china dogs sit
in dim silence behind windows.

Ghosts of houses I once lived in,
float through my thoughts like moths –
home is minutes away: the kitchen
with spices; bed softness; paperclutter;
my partner filling his computer's blue sky
with symbols; seedlings on the landing sill.